INTRODUCING THE STAR OF THIS BOOK

★ TRICERATOPS ★

(try-SAIR-uh-TOPS)

DID YOU KNOW...

that *Triceratops* has one of the largest skulls of any land animal that has ever lived. The largest was over 2.5 m long!

Triceratops means 'three-horned face'

SETTING THE SCENE

It all started around 231 million years ago (mya), when the first dinosaurs appeared, part-way through the Triassic Period.

The Age of the Dinosaurs had begun, a time when dinosaurs ruled the world!

Scientists call this time the

MESOZOIC ERA
(mez-oh-zoh-ic)

and this era was so long that they divided it into three periods.

TRIASSIC
lasted 51 million years

JURASSIC
lasted 56 million years

252 million years ago

201 million years ago

Triceratops lived during the Cretaceous Period from 68 – 66 million years ago.

CRETACEOUS
lasted 79 million years

145 million years ago 66 million years ago

WEATHER REPORT

The world didn't always look like it does today. Before the dinosaurs, and during the early part of the Mesozoic Era, the land was all stuck together in one supercontinent called Pangaea. Over time, things changed and by the end of the Cretaceous Period the land looked like this.

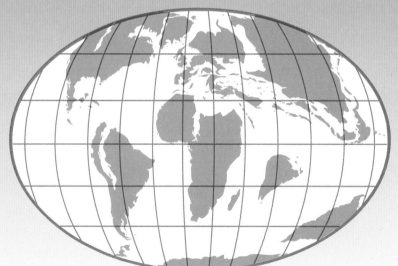

CRETACEOUS 66 MYA
Name comes from the Latin word for 'chalk'

TRIASSIC

Very hot, dry and dusty

JURASSIC

Hot, humid and tropical

CRETACEOUS

Warm, wet and seasonal

During the Cretaceous Period the continents separated further and the world looked almost like it does today.

HOMETOWN

Here's what's been discovered so far and where...

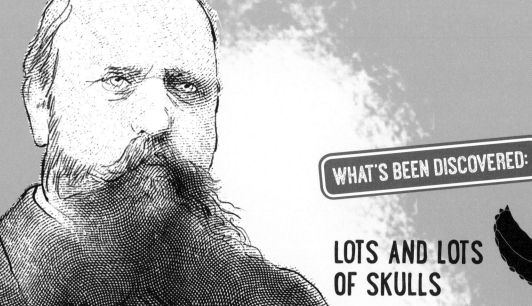

WHAT'S BEEN DISCOVERED:

LOTS AND LOTS
OF SKULLS

PALAEONTOLOGIST
OTHNIEL CHARLES MARSH
NAMED TRICERATOPS
IN 1889

WYOMING

USA

AND SKELETONS!

In 1887 a partial skull with horns was found in Denver and sent to the famous palaeontologist O. C. Marsh to study. He mistakenly identified it as belonging to a prehistoric bison, a type of buffalo.

However, it was not until Marsh studied another partial skull from Wyoming that he realised his earlier mistake. Remains of *Triceratops* have been found in several states in the USA and also in Canada. *Triceratops* skin has been found too!

VITAL STATISTICS

Ceratopsian dinosaurs typically have beak-like mouths and bony crests. Lots of ceratopsians have been found around the world. Some of them were small, but *Triceratops* was the largest of them all!

Let's look at *Triceratops* and see what's special, quirky and downright amazing about this dinosaur!

TRICERATOPS

3 m tall from toe to hip

The longest *Triceratops* skull found is over 2.5 m long, which makes up almost one third of their body length. *Triceratops* would need three doors side-by-side, just to fit its head through!

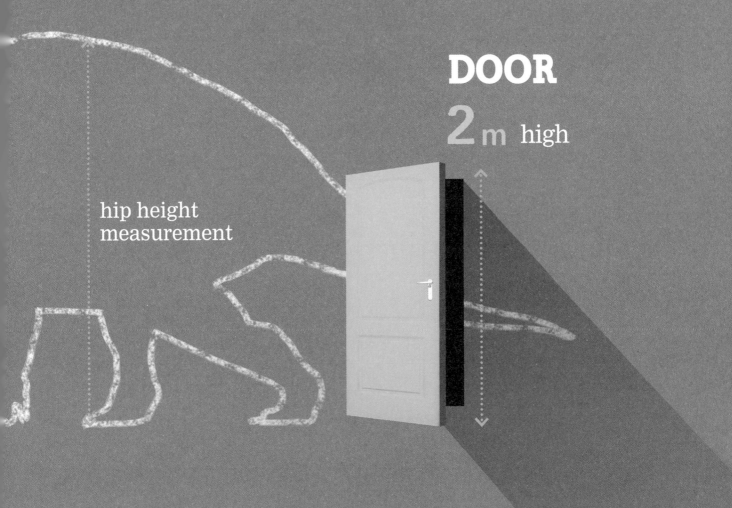

DOOR

2 m high

hip height measurement

TRICERATOPS

Length: **up to 9 m**
Height: **3 m**
Weight: **8 tonnes**

MOUSE

With a similar gait (way of walking) and horns used for defending and attacking, *Triceratops* is often compared to a rhinoceros!

Both have solid, heavy bodies and thick, strong legs and can move surprisingly fast when they feel threatened and decide to charge!

WHAT'S SO SPECIAL ABOUT TRICERATOPS?

WHEN TRICERATOPS LIVED

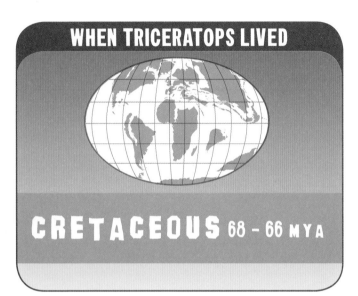

CRETACEOUS 68 – 66 MYA

TOOTH SIZE

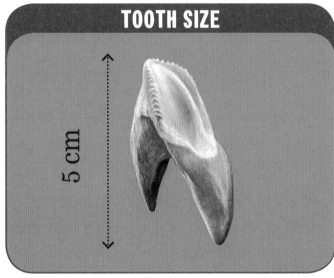

5 cm

WEIGHT

8 TONNES

FAST OR SLOW?

SPEED

out of 10

8

THE BEST BITS!

DISCOVERED, SO FAR

LOTS AND LOTS OF SKULLS AND SKELETONS

HOW FRIGHTENING?

SCARY

2	8
if chilling	if attacked

MEAT OR PLANTS?

SPECIAL BITS

HORNS AND FRILL

WHAT'S NEXT ?

MEGALOSAURUS
the first to
be named

LEAELLYNASAURA
long tailed,
polar herbivore

DIPLODOCUS
long-necked,
whip-tailed giant

COMING SOON

Velociraptor
turkey-sized, feathered
pack-hunter

Spinosaurus
large, semi-aquatic,
fish-eater

Brachiosaurus
heavy, giraffe-like giant

Maiasaura
motherly, duck-billed
herbivore

Join the 'What's So Special Club'

JOIN OUR FREE CLUB

 Download fun dinosaur quizzes and colouring-in sheets
www.specialdinosaurs.com

 Enter the exciting world of a 3D artist and discover how a 3D dinosaur is created and made to look real!

 Find out more about our experts and when they first became fascinated by dinosaurs.

 Who is Nicky Dee? Meet the author online.

 Join the club and be the first to hear about exciting new books, activities and games.

 Club members will be first in line to order new books in the series!

COPYRIGHT

ACKNOWLEDGEMENTS

Dean R. Lomax
talented, multiple award-winning
palaeontologist, author and science
communicator and the consultant
for the series   www.deanrlomax.co.uk

David Eldridge and The Curved House
for original book design and artworking

Gary Hanna
thoroughly talented 3D artist

Scott Hartman
skeletons and silhouettes, professional
palaeoartist and palaeontologist

Ian Durneen
skilled digital sketch artist of the
guest dinosaurs

Ron Blakey
Colorado Plateau Geosystems Inc.
creator of the original
paleogeographic maps

My family
patient, encouraging and wonderfully
supportive. Thank you!

To find out more about our artists, designers
and illustrators please visit the website
www.specialdinosaurs.com

BUS Traditional double decker

Length: 11 m   **Height:** 4.5 m   **Weight:** 8 tonnes (empty)

RHINOCEROS (male)

Length: up to 4 m

Height: 1.8 m

Weight: up to 3.5 tonnes

SCARY SCALE

How does *Triceratops* rate?

NOT SCARY

1   2   3   4   5

↑

Whilst
wandering
around and
eating.

When under attack!
If feeling threatened,
an adult *Triceratops*
would charge at its
enemy, head down,
ready to attack with
its horns!

6 7 8 9 10

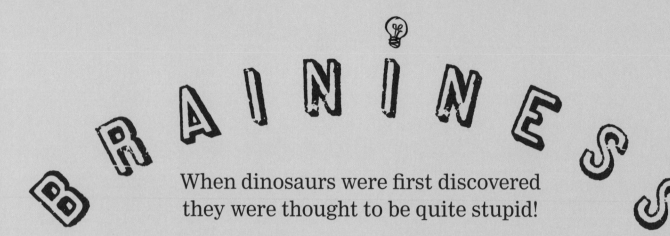

BRAININESS

When dinosaurs were first discovered
they were thought to be quite stupid!

Then a few scientists thought that some dinosaurs had
a second brain close to their butt! That's now just a myth.

Today scientists know that dinosaurs had one brain and were
intelligent for reptiles. Some were among the most intelligent
creatures alive during the Mesozoic Era, although
still not as smart as most modern mammals.

By looking at the:

Body size   Size
of the
brain   Sense
of
smell   Eyesight

scientists can tell how they rated against each other...

WHERE DOES TRICERATOPS, A PLANT-EATING DINOSAUR, STAND ON THE 'BRAINY SCALE'?

TROODON
(TRU-oh-don)

10/10
CARNIVORE
(brainiest)

T. REX
(tie-RAN-oh-SAW-russ rex)

9/10
CARNIVORE

IGUANODON
(ig-WAHN-oh-DON)

6/10
HERBIVORE

TRICERATOPS
(try-SAIR-uh-TOPS)

5/10
HERBIVORE

STEGOSAURUS
(STEG-oh-SAW-russ)

4/10
HERBIVORE

DIPLODOCUS
(di-PLOD-oh-KUSS)

2/10
HERBIVORE
(not so brainy)

These dinosaurs are drawn to
scale in relation to each other!

SPEED-O-METER

SLOW

① 1 ② 2 ③ 3 ④ 4 ⑤ 5

At full speed it is thought that a charging *Triceratops* would have been able to reach speeds of around 25 – 30 mph. That's very fast!

6 7 8 9 10

FAST

WEAPONS

The first thing anyone notices about *Triceratops* is the huge, bony frill on its head. Used for dominance, defence and display, these frills were massive and filled with blood vessels which lay just under the skin.

HORNS

The horns twisted and lengthened with age. A young *Triceratops* would have stubs that curved backwards, but as it grew they straightened, then curved forward, reaching lengths of up to 1 m.

Scientists think the horns were used for fighting off other *Triceratops*, as some fossil remains are damaged in a way that suggests that two *Triceratops* have locked horns in battle. Also for protecting itself from predators who thought it would have made a tasty meal!

BEAK

Triceratops had a toothless beak at the front end of its snout that was used to grasp and snap off plants. It was probably used for defence too!

SKULL

So many *Triceratops* skulls have been found in the Hell Creek Formation, Montana, USA alone, that scientists can study the differences between adults and babies. They now know that the horns and frills were not fully developed until adulthood.

TEETH

Triceratops had hundreds of teeth in its mouth, although only a small number were used when eating. The teeth were arranged in groups called batteries and set in columns. Once a tooth fell out it was quickly replaced by another.

These teeth had a razor sharp edge. When *Triceratops* chewed, it didn't grind its food like we do. Instead its teeth slid past each other in a vertical (up and down) slicing motion. These teeth and strong jaw muscles enabled *Triceratops* to slice through the toughest plants.

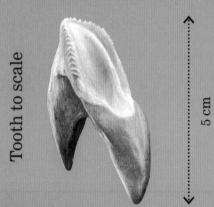

Tooth to scale

5 cm

Over-sized version of the tooth so you can see the detail

DIET

With such a heavy skull, Triceratops couldn't rise up on its hind legs, so it ate low-lying cycads, ferns, bushes and even early flowering plants. However, it was strong and heavy enough to knock over a tree to get access to the leaves at the tops of the trees if it felt like a change!

NEIGHBOURHOOD?

TYRANNOSAURUS REX

(tie-RAN-oh-SAW-russ rex)

Living in the same marshes and forests of what is now North America, *Triceratops* and *T. rex* would have probably met often.

Some horn and skull remains of *Triceratops* display evidence of battles between the two dinosaurs. One such specimen shows healed bite marks on the horn and frill made by a *T. rex*, which suggests that the *Triceratops* survived the encounter.

PACHYCEPHALOSAURUS

(pak-ee-SEF-uh-lo-SAW-russ)

Pachycephalosaurus was a 4 m long, dome-headed, bipedal (walked on two legs) herbivore that lived in the same woodlands as *Triceratops* and *T. rex*. Just like *Triceratops*, it lived in small herds. There was safety in numbers when T. rex was lurking about!

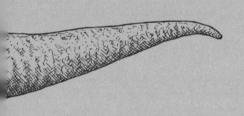